Soul Sounds

Reflections on Life

by Albert Micah Lewis

Albert M. Lewis
© 2009
COMMONGOOD PUBLISHING
Grand Rapids, Michigan

About the author

Albert Micah Lewis is a rabbi, writer, consultant on issues of middle aging and aging and professor of psychology and gerontology at Aquinas College in Grand Rapids, Michigan. His articles appear weekly in the *Grand Rapids Press* and his essays have appeared in several journals and books throughout the United States and Canada. Rabbi Lewis is married to Dr. Shirley K. Lewis and they are the proud parents of Julie Torem and Jamie Masco. Rabbi and Shirley are the "exceedingly proud" grandparents of Max and Ellie Torem and Jacob Aaron Masco.

This book is dedicated to Max, Jake and Ellie.

Table of Contents

Introduction

When I was a college student I often sat in one of the music listening rooms for hours on end. There, with Stravinsky or Vivaldi streaming through the ear phones, I would write research papers, explicate poetry and allow the music to become one with my body and soul. Years later as a rabbi and public speaker I wrote eulogies and inspirational talks that spoke to peoples' inner lives, losses and loves. Sometimes, after reading a draft of one of these pieces, I wondered where it had come from. Certainly, it had come from me, but it had also come through me—through my pain and joy, through my doubt and certainty, through my daring to dance with the Divine and to be open and vulnerable...open to hear, reflect, wonder and share.

The essays in <u>SOUL SOUNDS</u> are selections from more than three hundred articles written for my weekly columns in the Grand Rapids Press. They are glimpses into my personal journey, but they are also universal. My writing has been influenced by many philosophies and religious traditions as well as my own pain and passion.

This book is dedicated to my grandchildren, Max, Jake and Ellie. I love you unconditionally and fiercely.

(Writing essays and books is what Poppa does when he is not wrestling with you, making up word games and goofy rituals—or working). This, my dear grandchildren is some of what I feel inside. There is still much more to share with you and I will do so as you and I continue to grow.

Tim Smith of Schuler books has been a driving force in seeing that I produce this volume. Keith Longberg and Phil Jung have been wonderful friends, mentors and guides. My wife, Shirley K. Lewis continues to be my muse, editor and blessing. With her the journeys and sojourns in the heat of the desert and amid the cool breezes of the coastal cities have been life affirming and eternal.

I invite you to read the selections in <u>SOUL SOUNDS</u> in whatever order you choose and to reflect on the questions at the end of each piece. Please, write in the margins, circle words or phrases and make this book your own. My greatest wish is that <u>SOUL SOUNDS</u> will lead you into a greater appreciation of your life and experiences.

Morning Walk

—⟋⟋⟍—

God and I walk in the early morning. I take the dog along. God talks. I listen. The dog sniffs and pretends she can still hunt. We go early because God is busy; my joints ache if I don't move soon after arising, and the dog has needs to address. Along the way God points out the glistening dew or a large Tom turkey sauntering down the street, and, occasionally a reddish fox as it dashes across the road and into the woods. The dog plods on but looks back now and then as if to ask: "What are you guys talking about?" or "Are we almost home?"

When I come back from my walk I'm ready to "perform the duties the day." Undoing the dishwasher or folding a load of laundry—even paying a few bills—seems natural and life affirming. Along our walk God has reminded me I am fortunate to have clothes to wash and food to place on dishes.

God and I have reached an understanding. I speak late in the day through evening prayers. I can say anything I want; whatever I feel. He listens. In the morning He talks, tells me how to readjust my priorities—reminds me to call my father—and offers simple suggestions like: "Don't fret over writing a book; just write a chapter when you feel like it. Remember you are loved, healthy and able."

Walking with God is an ancient practice. It goes as far back as Noah. The text of Genesis 6:9 tells us: "Noah walked with God." That text also says Noah was a righteous person "in his generation." The rabbis suggest Noah was a pretty good guy when compared to many others of his time. He had faults, but they were relatively minor (at least in the early part of the story). Some traditions suggest Abraham was more righteous than Noah because he "walked before God, ahead of God." I have to admit I feel quite fortunate to get up in the morning to walk with God and Ruchi Marie (our dog). Sure, I would like to reach what the rabbis considered the higher plateau of Abraham—knowing what God wants before it has to be articulated; but I rather like the current dialogue and my incremental awareness. I don't want to be more like Noah or Abraham; just more fully Albert.

Sometimes I have to walk later than I might wish. There are immediate responsibilities, or ungodly weather. At times I'm too tired to absorb any more messages. Now and then I wonder what the response might be if I were to say: "Oh, I rarely attend early morning meetings; that's my time to walk with God!" So God and Ruchi and I walk. I listen to words and wisdom waiting to be shared. My inner world improves, the day goes on and at night I say: "Thank you, God. See you in the morning!"

Questions for Reflection:

How do you understand the phrase—"Walking with God?"

Is deliberate conversation with God part of your day? What do you talk about?

Zen PC

—⟋⟍—

I think my laptop is Buddhist; maybe even a Zen master. Sometimes, in my most intense moments of writing or editing, it winks at me and asks if I would like to condense the "data on my hard-drive." When least expected, it offers me the soul-cleansing opportunity to "move to trash" or even "delete" old files or outdated messages. And, every few months it quietly asks if I might like to "review old documents."

I hear my Zen PC whisper: "We know I have almost unlimited storage capacity, but how much of these bits and pieces do you want to carry around? They may be weightless, but sometimes they're also unnecessarily weighty."

And I begin my imaginary dialogue with Zen PC: "I brought you into my life to help me produce. Stop bothering me."

Zen PC replies: "If you reduce, you will produce. Inhale-exhale; import-export; sort." If I truly listen, something mystical occurs. Zen PC remains at 4.2 pounds, but my innermost hard-drive is lightened. Breathing, writing, feeling and acknowledging become easier, more natural. Concepts and concerns replace cleverly turned phrases; people and passion become the poetry of the moment, and I know the calm peace of simply being.

Unless someone like Zen PC (or One who loves us) interrupts our blinder trodden paths, our minds are likely to fill with phantom arguments, re-runs of old resentments, and we will waste too much energy and space with delusions worthy of deletion. Zen PC wants me to examine my personal files and carefully consider the messages I send. He is asking me: "If you could share one message with Eternity, what do you want it to be? If you intend the message to be from the core of your innermost processor, what must you edit, take to the thesaurus or delete?"

Next to my computer is this month's Discover magazine. When I took a moment to reflect on what I had written, I opened the magazine to page 15 to find the following research about reshaping the past:

"Every time a long-term memory or an associated emotion, like fear, is retrieved, proteins found in the synapses between neurons are degraded, allowing that memory to be updated by incoming information."

The article continues to discuss ways of reshaping our perceptions of the past, and ways in which obsessive and fearful thinking might be lessened. I wonder if the research scientist, Bong Kiun Kaang and Zen PC have met. Maybe I can find an e-mail for each of them and put them in contact with one another.

Questions for Reflection:

What messages from your past give you comfort and joy?

What messages are you ready to edit or delete because they are no longer useful to you?

Circle of Life

—◯◯◯—

It's just the way life is. The married daughter and son in-law come home to share their joy with her parents. They are pregnant and bring a picture, a sonogram of the child that is now enjoying its sixteenth week in the womb. The family celebrates, as does the extended family of friends. A baby is on the way. Grandparent-hood is coming. The rest of us have been there before and we share in our friends' joy. We understand their excitement and their often unspoken fears.

It's just the way life is. The pregnant daughter and husband, her married sister and brother in-law and her parents sit in a hospital room as the grandmother draws infrequent breaths and the signs of impending death are all too clear. They are all there to sing to her and comb her hair; to share their joy and their sorrow.

It's just the way life is. Soon the tiniest of critical or-gans will begin to develop in the grand-daughter's fe-tus; the heart and lungs, kidneys and all that will clarify and purify the flow of life. Less than five feet away the same organs are closing down in the grandmother and her once perky color is fading. We don't know what she hears at these moments; partly because of her severe hearing deficit, and partly because we just don't know. We know the fetus doesn't hear yet, though some may experiment with different music thought to sooth it.

It's just the way life is. An elderly woman will pass from one energy realm to another and will ask for nothing. And an energetic infant will emerge from the birth canal and demand every conceivable form of at-tention. We will ask God that this lovely woman rest in peace. And soon two frazzled parents will ask "for one night of peace." The dying woman, the baby wait-ing for birth and its parents are exactly where they are supposed to be at this moment.

It's just the way life is. A call will come soon and in one form or another the message will be: "I'm sorry, but Granny just passed away." Tears of sorry and relief will be reflected on the faces of the family. In a few months, another call will come and the message will be: "Mom, Dad, they're starting...My contractions are starting." And tears of joy and excitement will be reflected on the faces of the family.

It's just the way life is.

Questions for Reflection:

Can you recall the feelings you had when you first learned you were to be a parent or grandparent?

Can you write about some of those feelings?

The Emptiness

—⁓—

Many of the twentieth century philosophers, psychologists and theologians speak of a generalized sense of emptiness or incompleteness we all feel as human beings. While it has been given many labels (angst, anxiety, estrangement, detachment, anomie) it is real and lives within us; sometimes with a strong and strident voice we can hear...other times niggling just beneath the seemingly calm surface. It is, I am realizing in my journey through aging, a sometimes inexplicable sense of emptiness and insufficiency begging to be acknowledged; even filled. The issue that challenges each of us is not whether or not the barrenness exists, but how best to address it. When I have chosen to "fill the void," I have felt an immediate but temporary relief; and I have later realized I have to fill it yet again! I have purchased and consumed "things" that fill me... but only momentarily. When I have chosen to "feel the void," I have faced the recognition my world and my very being is not perfect, and that when I do feel the universal weariness and emptiness—in concert with all others—there can be a filling and feeling of being divinely connected to every one, everywhere. Einstein said: "Feeling and longing are the motive forces behind all human endeavors and human creations." And the writer of Genesis 1 reminds us that from the emptiness and void came physical and spiritual life.

On my journey I am understanding that the experience of being "alone" can be very different from being "lonely." More and more I am appreciating my alone time as "moments of creation," especially if the result of creation is a momentary calm I need only accept. And, in those moments, as Einstein understood, my longing leads me in to an acceptance of my humanity and that of others. From the "alignment of the alone" comes a true desire to interact in more open and direct ways. Perhaps Emerson said it best:

What lies behind us
And what lies before us
Are tiny matters compared
To what lies within us

We are, of course, shaped by what has happened to us in the past; some of it filling us in nurturing and life giving ways, and some leaving us with an inexplicable emptiness. What lies before us is dream. But what lies within us, if we choose to plumb the depths, are life and journey and awe and awkwardness and truths waiting to be shone in the light.

Questions for Reflection:

What are the times and experiences in which you feel "the emptiness?"

Who are the people and what are the situations that help you feel full?

Three Wise Men

—〰—

Three men sit for a meal. They rejoice in one another's health and camaraderie. They pray, eat and each shares a piece of his struggle. But each is more interested in talking about lessons learned from his youngest grandson. Three men bask in the joy that comes from inquisitive young minds and the delight of questions that send aging men to Google in search of adequate answers.

One grandson wants to know the names of the three magi. Another needs to understand the word 'voracious.' And the third wants to know how far he can push and rebel until there are consequences.

For over one-and-a-half hours, the men share their observations and amazement—even after they have long since finished their health-conscious meals and had more than enough caffeine for the day. They have errands, projects, appointments and tasks. But they will not leave without determining a date for the next "meal."

To the casual observer three men are eating, relaxing and sharing aspects of their lives. To the more trained heart they are rejoicing in values passed from generation to generation. These values are acknowledged through caring questions:

"Grandpa, why are there so many people standing outside (God's Kitchen) to get dinner, and how did they get here without a car?"

"Poppa, why would adults try to steal the golden ticket from Charlie (Charlie and the Chocolate Factory)? Don't they understand how hungry and poor his family is?"

Three men sit and smile because their children and their children's children have internalized the values spoken in the synagogue, church and mosque, but too often left in the parking lot. Three men eat carefully balanced meals because they want to live and see their grandchildren grow to adulthood. They want to know that in an unstable and uncertain world, religious values, caring for the "other" and questioning "what is" can stand against the cynicism and self-absorption of the moment.

In the New Testament, the names of the three wise men of the East are not given. We assume there were three because the story tells us about three gifts. In later Christian thought they are given names: Caspar, Melchior and Balthazar. And I wonder if they traveled together and, if so, what they talked about as they came to see the child Jesus. Maybe they talked about the values they hoped he would embody. Maybe they, too, were grandpas who wanted more for the world.

Questions for Reflection:

If you could offer or pass on three of your cherished values to your family or friends, what would they be?

For whom do you wish each value?

Have a Good Day

—ɯɯ—

"You have a good day." she said, handing me my coffee and change. "Thanks. You, too." I replied.

Sipping my coffee and exiting the store, a greeter also wished me a good day.

I walked to the car knowing that two perfect strangers had offered me a gift, and all I had to do was accept it and pay attention to the good I could give and receive.

Driving to work on a cold day with a hot cup of coffee was already an almost unnoticed "good." Walking into an editing and planning meeting with caring friends, I sensed I was with others who were committed to having a good day. An hour later, we produced a document superior to the one I had brought in, and we each walked away with the feeling—"This is going to be a good day."

Back in my own office, I began to work on some of the suggestions generated at the meeting: but, a moment later, I reached for the phone and called a friend who was recovering from her first round of chemotherapy. "I just wanted to see how you are, wish you a good day and hope that tomorrow is even better." At the other end, she offered a faint but appreciative: "Thank you. You have a good day, now!" I called to wish her a good day (which she really needed) and even with her compromised health and strength, she wished me the same.

Sometimes we forget the powerful and suggestive nature of words. None of us believes that a stranger wishing something good for us is going to make it happen. But, many of us believe that offering the right thought at what might be the opportune time can make a difference. And each of us will define what a "good day" is in our own way.

For one, it's making that sale and commission, and for another it's the ability to taste food again. In both examples, how the individual experiences himself and his surroundings will determine the ability to "have a good day." The sale is important because it confirms a sense of self (though narrow), and the taste of food is significant because it is one of the most basic of human pleasures.

A good day is not simply multiple satisfactions and interactions. Ultimately, it is measured in moments, inner movement and making decisions that matter. "Have a good day" can be understood as an empty business phrase, a command or an invitation. How we understand it will determine whether it will be a good day.

Questions for Reflection:

What makes a "good day" for you?

How do you help another to experience a "good day?"

Hearing God in Our Anger

—⁓—

My friend Barry called. It has been a difficult year for him, and he is punishing himself for not feeling more grateful and less angry.

Last fall, a drunken driver ran through a red light and hit Barry's car on the driver's side. Fortunately, Barry was more shaken than broken, but he has residual pain in his left arm. Recently, he was told the pain may always be there. The doctors tell him it's manageable, but it will be bothersome nonetheless.

In addition to this physical pain, his youngest son just left for college, leaving Barry and his wife adjusting to their empty nest. And the economy has made his already demanding and stressful job more so.

Barry tells me he feels selfish when he complains about his life.

"There are thousands of people without jobs, homeless people and kids without food. I have no right to complain," he says.

I asked if other people's plights would change if Barry chose not to express his anger and frustration.

We laughed.

We all have anger and frustration. It comes with living, and it's as normal as breathing as long as we acknowledge it and deal with it. I think we have a right to regret and none of us will get through life without driving on the avenue of anger. Many times, the avenue is a connecting road from a negative experience to a more positive one. And, sometimes, it feels like the only route, but it isn't.

Accidents, physical and emotional pain, difficult life transitions and daily stress cause multiple reactions. To feel anger does not mean we have to deny other emotions in our lives or in the lives of others. It does mean our sense of fairness, justice and right has been compromised with, and we don't like it.

I have lots of anger, and I try to leave much of it in the pool when I exercise. I also talk about it—when I am aware of it—and that helps. And sometimes it's just there, along with gratitude, wonder, love and fear.

There are certainly times when anger is appropriate and fully justified. William Blake wrote, "The voice of honest indignation is the voice of God."

The challenge you and I (and Barry) face is to know which anger is the voice of God and which is not.

Questions for Reflection:

Have you ever thought about putting your anger on paper?

What if you wrote down as many angry thoughts and memories as possible and buried them...or put them aside to read in two weeks?

Planning My Final Journey

—m—

A friend is planning her funeral. Neither of us expect it to be soon, or even within the next few years. But she is a practical woman with a tremendous sense of humor, an awareness of what is and is not within her control, and is very clear about what she does and does not want in life and death.

We lingered over lunch, talked about the world as it is, as we thought it was and as we wish it to be. We laughed, shared hurts and heights, and then she turned to me and said:

"I think you and I are almost talked out for today, so let me tell you where I need your help."

She began with a brief life review, which included real physical and emotional pain, and concluded with: "It's been a helluva good ride. Sure, there are things I would like to have been different, but if one of those changes took place, everything else would change, too. Now, let's talk about the service. Here's what I want…"

I know it sounds strange, and I do want my friend to live in health and peace for many more years, but I am looking forward to the funeral, too. It will be celebratory, borderline raucous, respectful, sad (because her children and grandchildren will lose one incredible mother and grandmother) and "just what the lady asked for."

The fact is, we are all going to die and many of us have an opportunity to decide how we want that death to acknowledge our lives. We plan and arrange so much of our living from long range retirement planning to dental appointments every six months and dinner dates on the weekends. I think we can derive great benefit and solace from planning our funerals, too.

For example, I don't want my funeral to be about "he did this and that," because most people who will attend the service already will know those details.

I want the funny stories and upbeat shared memories to be aired, exploits with my grandchildren retold.

I want one of my grandchildren to tell the story about Ellie and Max and Jake and the snake in the lake. I want a medium-grade cherry wood casket because I love good wood, don't want to spend money on the "Cadillac of caskets" and I want the least expensive grave liner.

If people want to speak, I want them to talk about me as a person who struggled with life and self-worth and acceptance and learned to laugh and share. Let them talk about me as a person who knew depression and exaltation, fear and occasional bravery.

And when all the "speechifying" is over, bury me next to the people with whom I have lived, loved, argued, laughed, cried and tried to share honestly since 1972. And then? Then eat, be loud and make big donations to the charity of your choice.

And on my headstone inscribe the following:

Albert Micah Lewis
Husband-Father-Grandfather
Great-Grandfather
Friend/Rabbi

Questions for Reflection:

If you could describe your life in ten words or less, what words would you choose?

Have you made your funeral wishes known?

Getting God
Out of the Margins

—ɯ—

The $1 coin, intended to replace the dollar bill has removed the phrase—"In God We Trust" from its central position. The phrase is still there, but on the side or "in the margins." Unintentionally, the coin reflects a reality in much of American life: The up-close and personal God often is found in the margins and to the left and right of what seems the norm. Religious institutions are struggling to attract people into their buildings; something more than Christmas, crisis and Yom Kippur.

On the exterior edges of these buildings, there is a clear message: "God may be found on the inside." But, too often when people enter, they don't find God in a way that is familiar. They find committees and causes in need of volunteers, music that may or may not help them transcend the moment, budgets in need of funding and the eternal question: "Where is everyone else?"

It is too easy to overlook the fact God is sitting in the next seat, wandering the hall in search of the adult education lecture, or sipping coffee, alone, in the corner. God sometimes is a little left or right of our expectation—there, but not as obvious as we might hope. The rabbis tell the following story:

In the late 19th and early 20th centuries, during the great anti-Semitic pogroms in Russia, one of the community leaders would go into the woods, light a fire, recite a series of prayers and plead for God to intercede. Intercession came. In successive generations, a leader would go to the woods, find the special place, light the fire, but forget the blessings. Finally, at the height of the hatred and killing, leaders from two communities went to the place, silently lit the fire and in great distress said to one another: "I know this is the place, and I know how to assemble and ignite the fire, but I don't know how to speak to God." And one turned to the other and whispered: "Maybe, if we talk to one another about our deepest feelings, maybe God will hear us and respond." That day, two men found

God in their mutuality and openness to one another. And God was in the center.

The open door of a synagogue, church or mosque is an invitation to meet others who want to kindle a very human and essential fire and who may not be sure how to do it. Like so many of us, they are seeking the connection, validation and reassurance essential to a healthy sense of self, personal value and dignity.

And every time we truly see another and tell her how good we feel to see her and to speak with her, God moves from the edges to the center, and trust builds and rebuilds. And "In God we Trust" moves from the edges and into our centers.

Questions for Reflection:

Can you describe the times or places where you feel most centered and able to experience God?

Are there certain people or patterns that make the experience easier or more difficult?

Winter Wonder

—∞—

If the white and wisps of winter's winds and the broad bland that bands the sky is seen as death, the Artist's desired depth is diminished. Below the snow and Earth's seasonal solidity, solitary seeds, ruminating roots and blooms beckoning blossom hold hope—and even more—a shared promise.

We who shovel, scrape, mumble and minister to the cold toes and reddened nose often miss miracles that lay below the surface; and we are dangerously distant from the Artist's intent.

The white we see is not an ending, but an ebbing.

It is like a beautifully iced cake viewed by a child for the first time. The child sees only the frosting and decorations, but knows little of anything below. That there is a cake beneath the frosting—substance under the fluff—is a revelation for the child.

Remember an early birthday cake of your own, to taste and feel and make into a mess? Remember touching it, molding it and even throwing it across the room?

Remember your first snow and the glee and unpredictability of it all?

"What is it?" you surely wondered.

"How did it get here?

"How long will it stay?

"What do we do with it?"

These were the questions of childhood

In adulthood, snow too often is the sign of a forced detour, away from the "out the door and on my way to more" way of thinking.

Instead, "slow down" seems to be the message. "Start earlier and go slow."

However, the Book of Winter's Wisdom says this: "Snowmen and snow angels, snowballs and ice forts, ice skating and sledding yield no product or income—only joy. If you dwell on what you cannot do, where you cannot go and that you must think about 'slow,' it will be a very long winter.

"But if you can choose to live well in 'the pause,' rest, refresh, reconsider and revisit your roots for tomorrow—not with giddiness but with an acceptance of what is—winter offers wonder, an invitation to let the heart and soul wander, a time to realign wishes and whisper "thank you."'

Questions for Reflection:

What is most wondrous about winter for you?

Do you remember a detour that took you to or through some place wonderful?

Stuff

—∿—

There is something about "stuff" that puzzles and frustrates me. While I know it does not multiply on its own accord, I seem to have an overabundance of it; and ridding myself of voluminous amounts of stuff seems to work for a very brief time.

Last week my friends from 1-800-GOT JUNK hauled away several boxes and an old treadmill, and I felt a few moments of "stuffus diminus." My basement area was certainly less cluttered, but my desk was now under siege from papers and unopened envelopes.

I decided not to bemoan my fate but to understand the reasons behind it. Was my affliction of "stuffus maximus" due to disorganization, insufficient room or some other causal connection? I decided to monitor myself at the market and at places where I might buy something because it was a bargain or an item "I will need eventually."

Do you know how difficult it is to go to the market and only purchase two items?

Shirley and I are working very hard to simplify and unclutter our lives. Various organizations are benefiting from our clothes and shoes. We take deep pleasure in looking into closets where each piece is in its place and there is a sense of roominess and air and "lightness of being." We tell one another that, at age 65, we are downsizing our debris and upsizing our inner being. Bunk!

In my head I have a list of the things, the "stuffus too-muchus" that I want to purchase in the next two years. The list, I have to admit, has nothing to do with need; it may, in fact, have more to do with greed.

Possessions can be wonderful when they serve a utilitarian or esthetic purpose. The art in my home office reminds me of special moments in my life. But the encyclopedia in my closet reminds me I have not used it in 10 years and all the information I need is online, Goodbye encyclopedia.

In October, we will travel to France. I am daring myself to bring back pictures and memories and very little stuff. Between now and then, I am throwing out more and more.

A Jewish maxim tells us we come into the world with our hands wide open as if to say:

"The whole world is mine, give it to me." It then says: "When we die our hands are closed as if to say: 'I have taken nothing with me.'"

I am not ready to die; but I am trying to live more intentionally.

Questions for Reflection:

Where is the clutter in your home?

Where is the clutter in your life?

What would you like to "clear out?"

Ballet of Balance

—〰—

Running late to attend the funeral of Monsignor Ancona's mother, I passed a large billboard that read: "Life is a temporary assignment."

The words stayed fixed in my mind for the rest of the day, and I commented to Shirley about them that evening. It was the idea of "temporary" that struck me so deeply—in one way awakening me again to life's brevity and the need to play along the way; in another way noting that even after more than 90 years, my friend's mother's life on Earth was temporary.

As I write I am able to give myself permission to enjoy the journey; but had it not been for the two signs—the billboard and the funeral—I think I would not have tried to slow down. When I do slow down, like many others I discover aspects of myself otherwise hidden or denied. I am beginning to enjoy simple but satisfying wood-working. I now own a supercharged drill and shelves—from a former closet—are appearing in our basement. Objects that formerly occupied the floor are on shelves, on hooks or in the trash. And, just like their owner, the old closet shelves have found a new role in life.

A friend has told me about a "temporary" teaching position she will fill in September. As we talked about her new opportunity to share her talents, we also realized that this "temporary" position might become "permanent." And we understood permanent meant "a longer temporary."

In wedding ceremonies some clergy ask the bride and groom to pledge their love to one another—"Till death do us part." In a sense, clergy are telling us that even the deepest and most significant relationships in our lives are temporary: and they are encouraging us to live them as fully, openly and robustly as possible.

You and I are engaged in a ballet of balance. We want to extract and impart as much as we can today while planning for tomorrow. It's a difficult routine, and it requires constant practice and refinement. Being too committed to tomorrow diminishes the possibilities of today. And, too much dancing today may cause anxiety and pain tomorrow.

Life is a temporary assignment with the potential for more now and later. Saadia Gaon (882-942) taught: "The Golden Mean is to love this world, to do good in life and to aspire to the world to come." If we all follow the Gaon's advice, our "temporary" assignments may bring great joy today and tomorrow.

Questions for Reflection:

How do you want to spend the rest of your "temporary assignment?"

What are some aspects of your "hidden" self that you would like to bring further into the light?

Magic and Mystery

—⚶—

I once asked a very talented magician how she did a particularly astounding close-up trick. "Very well," she replied. Though she was correct, I was disappointed with her response. I wanted to know the secret behind the magic. I quickly learned to accept the joy of the mystery, and years later to acknowledge mystery and awe as essential to my life. And now, as time (a mystery within itself) grants me the pleasure of revisiting philosophers, scientists and theologians shelved for forty years, I find myself sojourning with those who have preceded me on the journey.

One of my fellow travelers is Albert Einstein (who made me feel comfortable as a child with the name "Albert" when I would have much preferred "Ted" or "Bill"). With all of his scientific knowledge and acclaim, Einstein wrote poignantly about what he called a "cosmic religious feeling," In 1932, addressing a 6th grade Sunday School child's question about whether scientists pray, Einstein replied:

> "...every one who is seriously involved in the pursuit of science becomes convinced that a spirit is manifest in the laws of the Universe—a spirit vastly superior to that of man and one in the face of which we with our modest powers must feel humble."

Einstein did not believe in a personal God, an anthropomorphic judge, but in "a humble admiration of the infinitely superior spirit that reveals itself in the little that we, with our weak and transitory understanding, can comprehend of reality." He would go on to say that "morality is of the highest importance—**but for us, not for God**."

My own reading and reflecting on life beyond the immediacy of the moment allows me the freedom to wade through the wonders of life and to breath deeply inward the awesomeness and sometimes awfulness of life. For me, more so than ever before, the shared mysteries of life, ever changing as life itself, send me deeply inward where I re-discover a commonality with all life...and then outward where I am, for my own sense of wellbeing, compelled to share and become one with the awe. Religious literatures of **all** people instruct me on the sanctity of the primary search and the secondary importance of the answers. God becomes neither judgmental nor manipulative but the cohesive and collaborative mystery in which I—we—and all that exists become One. And prayer, which Einstein saw as "a wish addressed to a supernatural Being" becomes a means of unifying the individual with her deepest human convictions, the community with its most profoundly shared dreams and values, and our universal condition to understand the magic and the mystery. And if, at life's end I am asked to summarize all I have learned, I want to be ready to say: "Life is a mystery floating on a sea of awe and I swam in it…and was refreshed by its waters."

Questions for Reflection:

What do you feel you share in common with the entire world's people?

When and where do you feel and indefinable "Oneness?"

Be AWE-some

—〜〜—

Shirley and I sent Chanukah or Christmas cards to many family members. In each one, we wished them a "Happy New Year." But now I'm not so sure that's what I really want for them. Certainly, I don't want them to be miserable, but "blatantly blissful" is not part of my wishing either.

In the new year, I am hopeful those closest to me will be grateful for who and what they have, who they are and "how" they are living their personal and spiritual lives.

I wish them new questions and moments of self-doubt; the kind of doubt that challenges ways that have become too comfortable and leads to an awareness of "More." Yes, I want more for my family and friends (and self) but the more that results in AWE (awareness, wonder and enthusiasm for life),

AWE can enable us to hold a simple cup of hot tea and fully enjoy the steam, aroma, taste and warmth. No longer is it "just tea."

AWE can turn a long-distance conversation with a grandchild—however brief—into a miracle of time, technology and temperament. It wasn't very long ago that long distance calls were expensive, even a luxury. Now, for less than five cents a minute we can speak to one another anywhere in North America sometimes even with pictures coming through the internet. AWE raises our sometimes blase ordinary to the extraordinary.

In the new year, I offer you a gift that is priceless, yet not costly; precious, but not marketable; and singularly unique. I offer you the gift of your most AWE-some self. Accepting the gift requires only a decision and a slight change in perspective. You can try it out at no cost or obligation. Walk to the window and look out. If you see only limitations, look again at how the snow nestles in the boughs, rises and falls with the wisps of wind. Look into the mirror of your soul. See what is and what "wants to be born." Decide if you are ready for the AWE of birth. Be gentle to yourself. Remember, birth happens after a lengthy period of many small changes.

So, give yourself the gift of time, also.

Questions for Reflection:

What five wishes would you want for your family and friend?

What five wishes will you give yourself?

Mirrors

—⟋⟍—

It's mating season. Daily, a black bird with a brown head appears on our deck, looks into the kitchen window, puffs himself up and then sits. He repeats his "inflation infatuation" off and on for about an hour and then flies away. Shirley worried he was wounded. But, as she described the bird's behavior to a friend, she learned he was confused and probably thought he was "courting" another of his species. But he's courting himself! It's as though he looked into a mirror, saw another with the strengths he sought and the flaws he could tolerate and decided this one could be my mate!

In the mirror he may have seen what he lacked but wanted: a bird like him—an acceptable image of himself.

We are surrounded by mirrors. The most familiar hang on walls and doors. And the most significant mirrors are in the words, actions, body shapes and emotional makeup of those around us. I don't know "that overweight man" ahead of me in the checkout line, but I see my weight struggles in his heft. "Why doesn't he lose weight?" I whisper to my big body. "I hate the way the mother is verbally abusing her child." She reminds me of words I have sent and received.

If I could look into the "mirror, mirror on the wall" (and if it could talk), what might it say?

"There's a pimple on your face. It's not all of you—just a blotch in a small place."

"Sometimes, your words are like honey. They bring calm."

"Except when you bark and scream, prancing around…a silly, self-absorbed emotional bomb."

"You see big flaws in that other guy, though he might have something you can't buy. Maybe he knows what you see. And maybe he looks into the mirror and says: 'I'm not perfect, but I'm truly me.'"

"I bet he's working on his stuff; too busy to see the flaws in you. And, what if I told you he's mostly happy, too?"

The bird is back. He's puffin' and fluffin' again, and my attitude has changed, so I now can admire his persistence. I'm sending him a telepathic message and saying: "Step back from the mirror. Move away from yourself. You deserve more than an image. Go for the full life." And he starts to sing a song: "Life is with people, every shape and every size. Look at their faces and into their eyes. They want to connect, and they each have a song. Mirror their joyfulness, and we'll all get along."

I'm off to buy bird food. The sage at my window deserves a good meal. I will walk to the store.

Questions for Reflection:

Who do you see in your mirror?

What are his/her strengths-weaknesses, joys-sorrows?

Can you love the person in the mirror?

The Fog Lifts from the Water

—m—

From the window in my guest apartment, I could see the mist gently rising from the lake. The winds had created a small but rhythmic wave pattern and ducks were making their voices heard; calling for the full sun. Within minutes, the mist rose sufficiently to display the brightly leaved trees.

I recited my morning prayers and readied myself for a day of teaching, leading worship, tutoring and then dinner with friends. I was in Traverse City, ministering to the members of Temple Beth El.

I had prepared materials for my classes and the celebration of Sukkot, the fall festival. I had come prepared to address the needs of at least seven groups, bringing messages of continuity and reassurance. I had not anticipated a greater lesson was being prepared for me just outside my window. The lake and all of nature were my teachers.

Nature whispered softly to my soul: "See how the mist lies fog like on the water's surface? Notice how the sun lifts the mist and displays the leaves of fall. Do you see how even now the waters move and the fowl sing their hymns of praise?" And my soul, well before my mind, responded: "Yes, and thank you."

As I drove from the countryside to the city I saw the mist lifting from the fields of winter wheat and corn, and old barns in muted reds and greens. And they, too, spoke: "We have been here long before you and will probably be here after you are gone. We've seen it all, and we have survived it. We are just wooden beams and boards and bolts. Not very smart. Not too resourceful. But, like you, not alone."

My morning Torah students and I opened the first chapter of Genesis and read: "And the spirit of God hovered over the face of the waters. And God said: 'Let there be light.' And there was light."

The opening chapter of Genesis tells us the Earth was unformed and void. I understand that to mean nothing was organized, established or in its place. I also understand it to mean "a long time ago." Thousands of years have passed since the oral traditions of Genesis began. All six days of creation have been completed. There are lakes and fowl and trees bearing their own seed and countless years of the sun burning away the fog that covers our eyes and distorts our vision.

Today, the entire world is engulfed in a void and darkness. And, to countless people around the world, God is whispering: "Let there be light." And I believe the light will come. It will come first from within each of us, from the place where God has chosen to "live in your midst." Then it will come from outside, from the courts and weights and measures and leaders we have established. And, we will each look from our guest apartment window (for we are all guests), and the mist will lift from the lake and the beauty of every season of life will emerge.

Questions for Reflection:

What fog prevents you from seeing all of life's beauty?

Into which darkness do you want to shed light?

Hot Bagels

—⟋⟍—

The arrival of fall and cool weather transports me to a time in the 1950s when gas wars waged between service stations and prices were 15 to 18 cents per gallon.

On Saturday nights my father would drive to the bagel factory and purchase a dozen bagels, right out of the oven. I often rode along and participated in one of those lengthy nonverbal dialogues so typical of adolescent males with their fathers. It was punctuated occasionally by one of us pointing out the latest model Ford or Chevy as someone with more money drove past.

We were the people who drove used cars. But, on the way home, we were the ones with a dozen hot bagels; so hot we tried to time the drive so they would be just right and ready for butter to melt on their still-steamy insides.

Fall also was the time to take down screens and put up storm windows, each numbered for placement on the correct window.

By late October, my father made sure coal was delivered and dumped in the driveway close to the coal chute. We shoveled the coal into the chute and, after the furnace was stoked and burning in November, I would remove the clinkers and put them on the driveway for traction in winter.

In a house of fewer than 800 square feet, my parents raised four children. Behind the garage they grew corn and tomatoes.

We certainly were not poor. We were among the "lower middle class" folks who worked, cashed their paychecks and brought home money to be divided into envelopes to pay the gasman, milkman and insurance company.

We didn't know anyone who had air conditioning. One or two neighbors had electric fans. Usually, they were families of autoworkers who had better salaries —and sometimes bonuses.

That was 55 years ago. My siblings and I have moved up a step or two on the middleclass ladder. My father can still tell me what the cost of a dozen bagels was and that sometimes you got a 13th bagel for free.

The 1950s have come back to mind as I've thought about the current economy and the possessions I have accumulated. As much as I love my "things," I know they are not the important stuff of life.

I sit with my bride of almost 46 years, and we talk about where, when and what to cut back. We share memories and our deepest hopes and fears. We hug and wonder what stories we will live to tell in five years. Then we turn down the thermostat, put on a sweater and plan a "bring what you've got" dinner with friends.

We don't have to tell them to wear a sweater. They know.

Questions for Reflection:

Can you recall one of your warmest memories from adolescence?

Can you recall special family times and the tastes that gave you joy or the feeling of being loved?

Autumn Leaves

—ᨓ—

The colors of autumn's leaves touch me where I am most alive and awake.

In their own way, they whisper: "We are dying; yet we choose to flow with the wind and laugh at the harshness of the rains, dance on the wisps of time and then, ever so gently, fall to our fate."

And, even when they reach the grass or street, their colors draw the eye. Children run to capture them between sheets of waxed paper, or to frolic among them as if death, when timely, were to be celebrated. In my youth, we would jump in and out of the dead leaf pile, and squeal with glee.

Their death was our beginning.

In the late fall, we would burn well-dried leaves, listen to the crackle in their voices and imbibe the unmistakable aroma that conveyed fall had fallen and winter waited its turn.

We shuffled to school along streets strewn with leaves and kicked them into the air; sometimes wishing they would magically reattach to the limbs from which they had fallen. None of us knew which tree or branch or limb. And none of us had the power to reverse what was and is.

The leaves, I came to understand, knew their time and their season. And, one day, I would know mine.

So now I look for the streets with many trees; some with colorful archways inviting me and so many others to pass beneath their bowed heads as they give themselves to something more—and in the process create a beauty some see as messiness.

But life, I am beginning to understand is messy, too. To think otherwise is to miss much of its beauty. So, in reverence and gratitude I remember the time when leaves burned and chilled winds blew, and we listened to the sounds and warmed ourselves with yesterday's beauty. And there was always one tree with a single leaf that stayed until the weight of snow forced it down. And winter, with or without the official calendar began.

Life is cycles marked not by mandated dates and sanctioned seasons, but by memories embedded so deeply that at any moment we can recall a scent or taste or picture placed in the recesses of the mind. And then we smile or cry or both.

So many colors and so many memories and so many morrows. And, as the tree awaits the spring and its new life, so, too, must we who see what is and dare to dream about what will be.

Questions for Reflection:

Where are you in your life cycle and how colorful is your life?

What is your fondest memory of fall?

In the Vineyard

—᠓—

On a recent tour of the northern Michigan wine country, I came to a better understanding of God. It wasn't the wine; but it was the nature of wine.

As we visited various wineries, the vintners explained the complex processes by which selected grapes become wine. As we sampled some of those wines, it was suggested we pay attention to the different bouquets and tastes, such as the hints of green apples, peaches, chocolate and berries.

The more we came to understand the complexity of the wines, the clearer it became there were no apples or berries or peaches mixed in with the grapes. However, in describing the wine, it was necessary to draw upon metaphors and shared experiences to help us understand the complexity of what our senses were conveying.

When we try to talk about God, we are enhanced by our experiences, too. Yet, we are also limited by geography, climate, cultural beliefs and experience and language.

Because people speak, we ascribe speech to God. But "speech" does not mean speech as you and I might talk with one another. Rather, it implies God communicates to us. And, since we are a culture that prizes verbal and written communication, we ascribe written and verbal skills to God.

The wine experts also showed us how some wines have "legs." They were referring to a certain way in which the wine, when swirled, adheres to the glass. It was their way of saying: "This wine stands up and stands out in specific ways, as if it had legs."

We have anthropomorphized much more than God and wine in our lives. My father reminds me tomato plants "like" an acidic soil and that coffee grounds are "good" for them. He and I know the plant does not have likes and dislikes as you and I do. But again, our human limitations affect our perceptions of reality.

I often am asked the question: "Did God create humankind or did humankind create God?" My answer always is: "Yes!" Something we cannot truly comprehend on a scientific or intellectual level caused life to be. As a result, we have strived over generations to understand and relate to that Something in our limited but profoundly sincere ways.

God is as real to me as the love of my wife and family. Can one live without a relationship to God or without a sense of the More? Of course. But that life will lack the bouquet, and the legs will be wobbly.

Questions for Reflection:

Can you describe a time when God gave you "legs?"

With whom do you want most to walk in your vineyard?

A Father's Blessing

—⟋⟍⟍⟋—

As I write, my ninety year old father, Henry, the son of Jacob, sits with our aging dog and is absorbed in the Sunday morning news programs. At Shirley's prompting I have brought my father from Detroit to see our new house and to enjoy the success and happiness of his oldest son. He has come to Grand Rapids before, but not since we moved into the condo we designed and continue to reimagine. Poppa is here to see "the house," but also because I want his approval and to share our joy. And, I want his blessing.

In the new year I will be 65 and I still want my father's blessing. I want to hear and feel and know that it is mine...from him. I don't want an exclusive blessing; there is surely enough for my sisters and brother, too. I know I can live without it; but I would rather live within it. He has already told me he is proud of how I

77

am living out my life. And I know deeply how much he loves my wife and children and grandchildren. I know he loves me.

Is it foolish for a 65 year old son to want a special blessing from his 90 year old father? I don't think so. The Biblical Jacob blessed his sons when they were older and he seemed to understand them in ways they may not have understood themselves. And his blessing was one of praise and gentle criticism and insight that a son wants only from his father.

My father has few "things;" no physical treasures my siblings and I will share. He has some stock which he has already divided to be shared equally between his children. We are not waiting for it—and in fact would rather he enjoy his life as fully as possible—using up all his resources before he dies. But he does have an accumulated wisdom and gentleness that carries no pretension and little if any acrimony. He is concerned about the world and opportunities for his great grandchildren, just as my sisters and I worry about our grandchildren. He sees the strengths and challenges facing the offspring who may carry his legacy into the 22nd century.

Before I take my father back to his home in Detroit, I will ask for his blessing. I will sit with him and say: "Poppa, you have lived a long and sometimes difficult life. You know things I don't know and there are aspects of life you see more clearly than I do. Please, share these gifts with me and bless me with your very being. Help me, Poppa, to become more of the man I am intended to be."

And my father will have words for me. I don't know what they will be. But they will be his gift and blessing to me. And I will be grateful.

Question for Reflection:

Is there a blessing—an acknowledgement—you would like from your father/mother, living or deceased?

Is there a blessing you would like to offer your parent(s)?

God Wept

(A Meditation in One Syllable Words)

—⚥—

God sits with a pen and writes. The ink is black, though the choice would be blue. But blue could be seen as joy, and it is scarce. God writes, and tears stain the lined pad. The world, once lush and green, once full of hope—once held with love—is dark as the ink.

God looks and sees that Cain lives. He prowls the earth and, snake like, finds a place in this or that heart where he can eat the seeds of love and leave dirt and doubt.

God looks in each place where light might seep through a small crack. Will one or two or more stand and say:

"We, all of us—all whose hearts beat and whose souls still know truth—we are all wrong! We have lied, dropped our eyes, and said the words that rolled off our tongues like truth, but fell like dead leaves on a cold Earth."

"I am so sad," says God. "I want one of you to walk the Earth with me. If I could see through your eyes—eyes that do not see as I do—if I could hear with your ears—if I could know the world in the way you know it, then I might see what needs to be done. I can't change what is. With your help I can change what will be."

And God looks through our glazed and dimmed eyes; eyes that shun the moon as well as the sun; eyes that do not cry. And there God sees so much fear, and then hears:

"I need to take care of me and mine." "I'm just one man and I don't know what to do." "My life is too full and some days there's so much." "Do you know how hard real life is, what I have to do to make it?"

God speaks once more and feels His own pain and loss.

"Did you have your meal? Is your child fed? Do you have warm, clean clothes, a home?" And then: "Does your pet have food?"

These words pierce the cold of the man who now sits and weeps. "I have so much. I am so blessed. I have a home, food, health…I am loved."

God nods.

"Did you know you were blessed when your eyes were filled with fear?"

"No."

"And what does it mean now that you see with 'new eyes?' Do you know the phrase—'And the blessed will bless?'"

"Yes."

"Can you live in this way? Will you?"

And for the first time that day God knew hope, and smiled. And a tear rolled down God's cheek. A soft rain fell on a parched world. And light was seen.

Questions for Reflection:

How does fear keep you from the fullness of your life?

What fears would you like to cast off?

No Perfect Parents—
No Perfect Children

—⚏—

My friend Susan recently shared an experience with me. She told me that after her parents had retired, they moved to a retirement community in the Los Angeles area. There they enjoyed the weather and intellectual stimulation until they became frail, and her father died. Following his death Susan made more frequent trips to see her mother and to oversee many of her medical and legal needs. In her own middle aging, Susan had worked hard to put her relationship with her mother into perspective and to forgive what ultimately must be forgiven. One night while in Los Angeles, Susan and her mom had a light evening of comfortable mother-daughter conversation. Mostly they talked about Susan's children and the life Susan and her husband were now living. As they prepared to go to their rooms for the night, Susan turned to her mother and said in a light hearted and caring way: "I want you to know that I have forgiven you for not having been the perfect mother." Her mother, who was now rising from her chair, walked slowly toward her own room, turned around and said: "I've forgiven you, too." When Susan shared this story with me, she told me how easy it was to see her mother's imperfections, but she had not expected her mother to acknowledge that Susan too, had made mistakes. Mom was not the perfect mother, and Susan was not the perfect daughter. And, in fact, none of us ever are!

All human relationships have flaws; siblings, partners, friends and parents—not to mention neighbors and acquaintances. One of the challenges of middle aging is to acknowledge our own limitations and to claim them as real. Of course, it is easier for us to see these shortcomings in someone else, especially a parent. Susan and her mother exchanged a wonderful gift —and they did so in a caring and non-confrontational way. It was almost humorous. Susan stated her truth to her mother without expecting anything in response. Yet, in return, she learned that she was not the perfect daughter; and she came to understand that too, was alright.

Sometimes adult children and parents place such high expectations on one another, and on themselves, and they cannot possibly be achieved. If I could live my life over, there are many things I would do differently with my wife, children and parents. I know that now because as a middle aged adult I have lived long enough to see and know alternatives that I earlier could not appreciate. That's normal growth and adulthood.

Many different religious traditions tell us how we are to act as children and adults; the roles of honor, respect and caring. The traditions share these insights with us because how we should act and interact is not self evident to any of us. We are all learners, students and people trying to do the best we can. Interestingly, none of the traditions tell us to be perfect or unforgiving or closed to new insights.

If you choose to speak with your aging parents or middle aged children as Susan and her mother did, there are some important guidelines. Remember that the goal is to open up communication or to expand it. This is a time of healing and growth and not a time to dump the excess hurt you have been carrying around. That baggage can be shared with close friends and professionals. If you want your older mother to know you are hurt because she never came to visit you in your new home, you might begin this way: "Mom, I have a beautiful home and family and I am sad that you were not able to come to visit us all these years. I wanted very much to share my joy with you. I used to be angry, but now I just want to talk and try to understand. When you are ready, could we talk about this?"

If you want your middle-aged son to know you wanted him to call or visit more often, you might say: "I always hoped that you would call me more often and come to see me more frequently. But I really don't know all the demands on your time or if there were other reasons we might talk about. When you're ready, I'd like to talk to you about these things."

Each is demonstrating the caring and consideration he or she wants from the other. An opportunity for new dialogue has been presented, and important healing may follow.

Questions for Reflection:

Are there issues or concerns you want to discuss with your parents/adult children?

Can you think of caring and non-threatening ways to discuss the issue/concern?

Facets of Time

—◡◡—

There is no such thing as time. And, according to the ancient Hebrews, there is no such reality as the future. For them, by the evidence supplied through the language and grammar, there was the past, the present and the imperfect-the "not yet but we hope and work toward." "Time," wrote one aging man, "is what you used to have a lot of, seem to have less of—except when you have too much—and yet invest in and plan around as if it were life."

In the winter of 2009 I tasted the sweetness and tartness of time. We were able to leave the snow and cold for a "period of time" and travel to Florida. In the first few days of our measured days away, we tried to pack as much life, levity and leisure as possible into "time." Later, we would recognize that what seemed like a "must" today could wait until "tomorrow." And, still later, after a series of tomorrows, there were fewer "times" available before we would go north, again. And then we woke up to a new truth. Time, like diamonds, would be multifaceted.

Diamonds have a high value because they are few in number, and the most valuable ones are limited. Mostly, though, they have value because they are markers of some aspect of a life event framed in time. You can sell, collect and negotiate with diamonds. It works with time, too, though a little differently. You can buy and sell cards with phone time, and if you take the expressway you might "save" time…which means you get to have more of it somewhere…and the best part, you get to have more of it with someone else.

We started getting up earlier and going to bed later and filled the day with more talks and walks, reading and writing, real quality "time" together. We made plans with friends to "share" time and realized—again —that sharing time multiplies it; even though it would seem to divide it. We talked of love and regrets and plans and fears and filled the air—and the time—with truths and words that sometimes are pushed aside by the snow plows and shovels in our lives. And we made a promise…about time. We promised to share, to savor and to laugh openly and frequently at the "same time next year." It's a long time from this time to that time,

so we have promised one another to "plan around it as
if it were life," because it is.

Questions for Reflection:

*Diamonds have many facets. You also have many
wonderful facets. Can you allow yourself to list
or consider some of them?*

*With whom do you want most to share time? Will
you?*

My Executive Assistant

——⟋𝍇⟍——

When adults allow the "inner child" to play, the whole world smiles. This became clear when I gave my youngest grandson, then 5, a small attaché case that formerly held 12 cigars. The aluminum case was far better than the cigars and an ideal size for a junior-junior executive. While visiting his Bubby (grandmother) in the hospital (a truly boring experience for a 5 year old) I presented the case to Jacob and told him he was now my executive assistant. He was thrilled and eager to know what that meant. "You will represent me at meetings I can't get to," I said. My Jacob was up for the task. "But Poppa," he observed, "I need a pen and some paper!" We went out to the nurses' station and I introduced Jake to one of the nurses. "This is my executive assistant, Jacob Masco. Could you give him a pen and some paper, please?" The nurse's inner child was as ready to play as was mine and Jacob soon had his pen, several sheets of paper and a few paper clips. He was also ready for a snack.

We went to the Blodgett Hospital gift shop and I again went through the introduction with the playful volunteer at the cash register. I shared with her that: "He will need to set up a charge account for peanut butter crackers and occasional candy...just in case he has to miss a meal on his way to a meeting!" She knew the game and asked if Jacob could sign his name. He could and did and "the account" was established. Jake placed his "necessities" into the attaché case (I paid the bill) and we were on our way back to see Bubby.

When Jake explained his new position to Bubby and showed the content of his case, she asked if he had a credit card. "Every executive needs a credit card," she advised him. "It helps you keep track of business expenses and deductions." "Oh," said five year old Jake. Shirley handed him an expired beauty salon gift card, and it was quickly placed in the business case. Later that day he and I went out for dinner. I suggested we split the bill, half on his card and half on mine. When the waitress brought the check I asked her to split it two ways and we gave her the two "credit" cards. She smiled and returned with two bills. Jake's was one half of the total bill which she had given to me. We signed the receipts, but not before Jake had one more question: "Poppa, how much tip should I put down?" (Jake's father is in the restaurant business) I suggested 20% because she had been very helpful (and playful). Together we figured out what 20% was.

At home before bedtime we ordered business cards for Jacob Aaron Masco, Executive Assistant. In my prayers that night I thanked God for adults who can allow themselves to be childlike. We need more such people and opportunities.

Questions for Reflection:

How and when and with whom are you most playful?

What pleasant memory do you have of a grand-parent?

Share My Peace

—⚏—

It was a Christmas card sent to us by a dear friend. The front was a picture of the Blessed Virgin and Jesus. We are Jews. My friend knows this. The card was beautiful; the true message, more beautiful.

I don't remember the words inside the card. I do know the words within my friend's heart:

"I am a committed and practicing Catholic, and I want to share my joy and peace with you. We are friends on different paths to the same One. Share my peace. Follow your path."

I could have wondered why he had sent us such a "religious" card, but I knew why.

Like so many others, we receive a number of holiday cards. Most have a generic seasonal theme, and the message seems to be: "We're thinking of you, too, at this season."

Christmas is a time of year when many people feel clearly included or excluded. It's wonderful to note how the "included" choose to reach out to those who may feel excluded or at least "not fully part of it."

It is also an invitation to examine our own belief systems and to do so honestly.

It's easy to talk about what we do not believe, but how many of us are ready to discover and discuss what we do believe?

In Hebrew, the words for truth and belief are derived from the verb "AMN," which eventually becomes "Amen" or "this is the truth I speak and affirm."

Before the New Year dawns, I invite you to begin your own examination of ultimate truth. Are faith, prayer, religiously based practices and celebrations, church, synagogue, mosque and community central to your life? Are you a "revolving door believer"— in on Christmas and Easter, Rosh Hashana and Yom

Kippur—and out for the rest of the year? Are you a "crisis Christian" or a "justifying Jew?"

Are clergy in your life or called in when you no longer know what to do? Is prayer part of your daily life? How often is your prayer one of gratitude and thanksgiving and how much of it is—"God, don't let me down."

The picture of the Virgin Mary and Jesus is beautiful. My mind's picture of my friend's outreach and caring is more beautiful.

May you fill your New Year with caring acts and caring people and with an openness to the One who whispers—"I am here."

Questions for Reflection:

Can you write down three-five beliefs that are central to your life?

Are you open to the beliefs of others?

In the Moment

—ɯɯ—

I have read and written much about living in the moment, but only recently did I realize how difficult this joy/pain can be. Vacationing in 85-degree weather in idyllic surroundings with wonderful companions I felt a new stress emerge. It chided and tormented me, and said: "You think because you have worked since you were 12 you may now bask in the rays of the Southeast sun...you think because your columns are written, your taxes are paid and you and your wife are in good health...you think you can now live in the moment? Think again, buckaroo!"

And I began to question how long I could find meaning in long early-morning walks, water aerobics and time to leisurely read four books—one in almost every room. How long could I sit with my wife and almost daily examine pain from a shared past and dreams of next year?

I tried to stay in the moment but found that, without some sense of more, without some sense of reality to force me beyond myself and my carefully conditioned continuum, the moment could become meaningless rather than meaningful.

It soon would become apparent that living in the moment requires an appreciated and shared past, as well as a sense of future. The future would be fluid and formless other than in words and wishes; but it would be there—here—beckoning.

Truly, moments are shaped by the experiences that precede them and by the feelings and actions that follow them. One moment may be contained in a frame of pain and disappointment, but when taken from its frame may bring both light and lightness. It does not disappear. It shapes the life of the next moment.

Moments can be released, reframed and the life force within them can be re-ignited. Living in the moment is joyous and painful, enriching and depleting.

Moments, like the art of the great masters, must be examined carefully and tactfully.

They are more than glimpses of what was; more than well or poorly chosen colors and strokes. They are three and four-dimensional artifacts of our lives inviting us to a showing of who and what we were and are.

Questions for Reflection:

What helps you live most fully "in the moment?"

What was the best moment for you today?

Silence and Joy

—〰—

Once I feared silence; I would quickly fill it with words or background sounds.

I have grown to appreciate silence and its role in my inner life. In the silence I can pray. Sometimes, if I stay within the quiet, I am able to hear my prayers and the responses that come forth from that "still small voice."

Even now, after all these years, if there is "too much" silence between us, I check with Shirley to make sure we are all right or to explain my own quietude. Sometimes, we share a place of silence and other times each of us must go there alone, usually to return more whole.

Driving home from three days with the grandchildren we each entered our sacred silence. For three days, we had played and joked, watched each child perform and had individual time to "just be" with each of them. The laughter was at times deafening; and sometimes just a slight motion reminded one or more of us about a joke we had made up and spontaneous laughter filled the house.

After all the good-byes and wonderful hugs, we entered the car for the six-hour ride home. Shirley and I shared a few words about the time we had spent (more like invested) together, then she turned to finish the book she was reading. She had less than 10 pages to go and wanted to finish before we were catapulted back into the daily routine. I am delighted when Shirley finds such solace in her reading; and I too, was ready for my own quiet.

Within my quiet, I reflected on so much that was said or seen, the growth of the grandchildren, their individuality, the evolving lives of my daughter and son in-law, the shared meals. I reflected on the blessings unfolding before my eyes—blessings that each carried the message: "Poppa (Bubby), come be part of my life, and I will enhance yours. I love you, and I know you love me. Just be with me and all of us will rejoice, even in the silences."

Shirley finished her book and I turned and asked: "What was the best part of the three days for you?" And together, after the silence, we recaptured the joy and laughter, spoken and unspoken messages. Soon we would place a talking book into the CD player. But first, we appreciated the silence of togetherness and the shared journey homeward.

Questions for Reflection:

When and where do you make quiet time in your day?

How does your quiet time enhance/diminish your life?

Happy Fathers' Day - 2009

—ɯ—

He looked up from his lunch, smiled and said: "I did keep you out of the factories." The thought had registered as deeply as I had hoped. The words had become Poppa's. I continued to enjoy my lunch and the moments with my soon to be 93 year old father.

I had driven to Detroit to thank my father, to acknowledge my own growth and our mutual successes. I wanted him to know that his hours of quizzing me for organic and inorganic chemistry and Latin had led me into a life of teaching and writing and great happiness.

He had forgotten I was coming. Even when I called from the car to say traffic was heavy and I would be a half hour late, it didn't all register. At 93 some things stay in the mind longer than others. The past may be more vivid than the present. I know and accept this reality.

At his home before lunch, Poppa asked if I had come to Detroit for a funeral or lecture. I smiled and said: "Poppa I have come to thank you and to take you to lunch." "For what?" he replied. "I want to thank you for guiding me, Poppa. I'm 67 years old, healthy, happy, successful in all the important ways...and I want to thank you. You encouraged me and you helped me to see there was a better path for me; the one that had not been open to you."

At age 93 schedules and routines are very important to my father. They are increasingly important to me, too. He had arranged to have his hair cut at 2:00 with his 88 year old brother. As we finished lunch I asked: "Is your barber near by? I could take you while I'm here." Poppa thanked me and replied: "I'll call George when we get home. We can still go together." I knew my offer had been heard and appreciated but there is a pattern, even a ritual between the two remaining brothers, and it needed to be recognized and respected. We went back to Poppa's place, talked for awhile and I left. There was still time for him to call George and to go to the barber.

On the ride home I thought about stopping at one or two specialty stores to purchase items I can't find in Grand Rapids. But, as I approached the stores, I chose to pass them. Their wares were tempting, but not necessary. I felt filled and content, heard and understood. It was time to go home.

Pavarotti and Vivaldi would accompany me on my return, and I would share my day with Shirley at the Shabbat table. In my evening prayers I thanked God for the opportunity to share my gratitude with my father. I think God smiled.

Questions for Reflection:

Can you write down the names of some of the people who helped you become the person you are today?

Can you write down one or two life-lessons learned from your father/mother?